Living Like Him

Ron and Rebekah Coriell

Published Under Arrangement with
Fleming H. Revell Co. by

A publication of
ASSOCIATION OF CHRISTIAN SCHOOLS INTERNATIONAL

P.O. BOX 4097, WHITTIER, CA 90607

Self-Control
bowl

Doing Something Even When I Don't Feel Like It

And every man that striveth for the mastery is temperate in all things. . . .

1 Corinthians 9:25

Self-Control in the Bible

At nine o'clock in the morning, a crowd of angry people brought Jesus to a hill outside the city, to be crucified. Jesus was laid upon a large wooden cross, with His arms and legs outstretched. The soldiers offered Him something to drink, which would deaden the pain. Jesus knew the suffering He would need to endure, but He refused the painkiller. What self-control!

Nails were driven into His hands and feet. Great pain filled His worn body, as Jesus hung before the onlookers.

"Father, forgive them," He said. "They know not what they do."

Before Him stood those whom He had created. Now they were crucifying their Creator. The crowd mocked and jeered Him. Jesus could have called upon thousands of His angels to rescue Him. Yet He knew He must suffer and die for the sins of the world. Thus He continued to allow the torture, even though His body cried out because of the pain. What amazing self-control the Lord possessed.

During the suffering, He spoke only words of mercy and kindness. That day Jesus took the punishment for our sin. Now, our resurrected Saviour offers eternal life to those who believe in Him.

Self-Control at Home

Thelma was busy helping her parents weed the garden, when she yelled, "Help! Help! A bee is flying around me!"

"Don't move," answered Father. "It won't hurt you, if you sit very still."

Soon, the bee left. Slowly, Thelma moved from plant to plant. Whenever she saw a bee, she jumped and ran to the end of the garden. Her parents noticed that she was not using self-control. Her father called her to his side.

"Thelma, you aren't remembering that I told you to be still when you see a bee."

"I know, Father, and I am sorry. It is because I am afraid of the bees."

Father replied, "Even though the bees are nearby, you must not run. They won't bother you, if you stay calm. Do you remember Philippians 4:13? It says, 'I can do all things through Christ which strengtheneth me.' Jesus can give you the self-control you need."

"All right," she answered. "I will do better this time."

Each time a bee flew past Thelma, she asked God to help her not to be afraid. So Thelma prayed, pulled weeds, and used self-control. Soon all the weeds were pulled.

Self-Control at School

"I didn't do it," argued Dick.

"Nevertheless, you must suffer along with the rest," said Mrs. Randell, the teacher.

There was a problem in Thelma Johnson's class. Some items had been stolen. Now, Mrs. Randell was making the whole class stay in from recess, until the stolen items were returned. It did not seem fair to Thelma for her teacher to discipline the whole class for the sin of one person. Then she remembered her Sunday-school lesson.

She had studied the story of Achan's sin. God had punished the entire Hebrew nation for one man's sin. That didn't seem fair, either, but Thelma knew that God does not make mistakes. She also knew Mrs. Randell loved and cared for all her students. Yet it was still hard to control herself while sitting inside during recess.

During lunch, some of Thelma's friends spoke to the person they knew had taken the items. He returned them later that afternoon. Mrs. Randell was glad to get them back, but she was even more excited that the class had encouraged the person to return them.

Now, Thelma realized why her teacher had made the entire class suffer. They were forced to help one another to do right. And Thelma was glad that she had the self-control to keep from getting angry with her teacher.

Self-Control at Play

"Let's go to the museum," said Frank, who was visiting his cousin, Thelma.

"No, let's go to the zoo," said Thelma. "I have been to the museum many times."

"But your cousin has never been there," said her father. "I am sure that he would enjoy seeing all those stuffed animals."

"Live animals are more fun to see than dead ones," pleaded Thelma.

"Yes, but Frank lives near a zoo in San Diego. He has never seen a museum like ours," Father said. "There are old airplanes, a big model-train set, and lots of old cars to see, too. I think it would be best to go to the museum. Let's get ready to go."

Thelma was sad. She did not get her own way. She just knew the museum would be boring. She felt like pouting and staying sad during the whole trip. Yet she also knew that would make four other people very unhappy: Mother, Father, Frank, and her heavenly Father.

It took a lot of self-control to smile, act interested, and try to be happy. As the afternoon passed, it became easier. Near the end of their tour, Thelma was happy that they had gone to the museum.

On the way home, her father whispered in her ear "Thanks, Thelma, for doing something, even though you did not feel like it."

Order

mortar

Everything In Its Place

Let all things be done decently and in order.

1 Corinthians 14:40

Orderliness in the Bible

Jesus had taught the crowd all day. Everyone was tired and hungry. The disciples suggested that the people be allowed to go into nearby towns and eat.

Jesus said, "Give them something to eat."

The disciples were amazed. Jesus had just told them to feed over five thousand people. Where would they find so much food?

Jesus asked, "How many loaves do you have? Go and see."

Quickly, they searched for food. Soon they came back with five loaves of bread and two fish. They wondered how so little could feed so many.

However, Jesus had a plan. He commanded the multitude to sit down in orderly groups of fifty. This way, it would be easier for them to be served by the twelve disciples. Then Jesus prayed and handed out the food to His helpers. There was enough to feed everyone. It was a miracle!

When everyone was finished eating, all the leftover food was collected. The food filled twelve baskets. Jesus made a big job easy, because He had everything done in an orderly way.

Orderliness at Home

"Father, come quickly," shouted Gordon, staring out the window.

"What's happening?" asked his father, as he came into the room.

"Look out the window, and you will see," Gordon replied. A spider was carefully weaving a large web. "It's as if he knew we were watching. Look how tiny those threads are. How can he do that?"

"Well, Son," replied Father, "The spider is one of God's most orderly creatures. He made them so that they could build their own houses out of the tiny threads you see. Each thread is made out of silk and is very strong. It comes from inside his body. See how orderly he is in making his web. Each thread must be put in just the right place, so that the wind and rain will not break it. This reminds me, Son. Did you know that children can be orderly, just like spiders?"

"How's that?" asked Gordon.

"Just as spiders have orderly houses, children can have orderly bedrooms. Have you put everything in its place, Son?" asked Father.

"No," he replied, "I guess I haven't. But if a spider can be orderly, so can I." Off Gordon ran, to straighten his room.

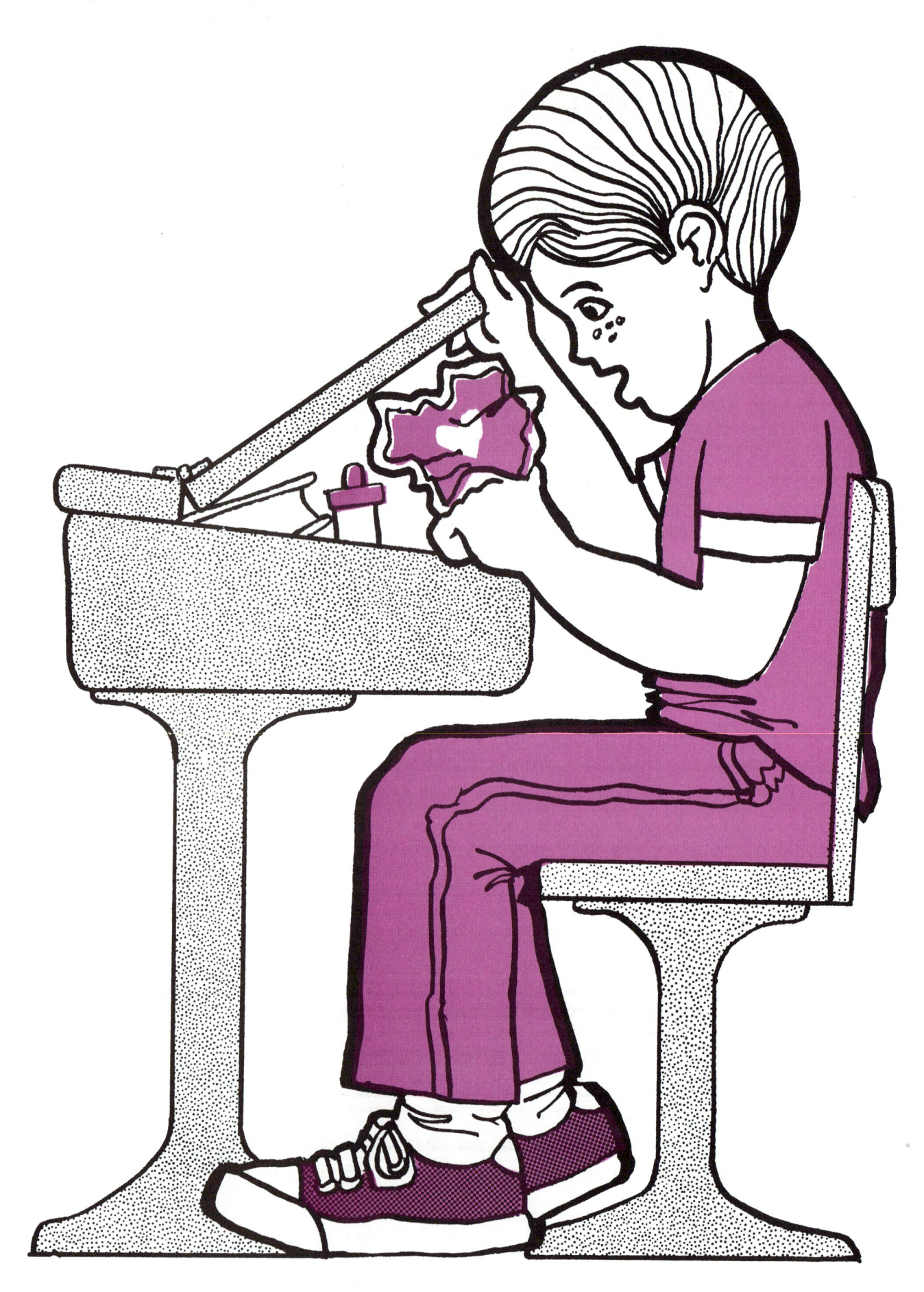

Orderliness at School

"Gordon, you always have such a messy desk," said a classmate.

Gordon didn't care.

With a look of unconcern, he replied, "I know it. I just don't have time to put everything in its place. Besides, I am busy making this valentine's gift for my mother."

Carefully, Gordon cut red paper into the shape of a heart. Next he cut a larger heart from white paper. He glued the two hearts together so that a little of the white heart showed around the edge of the red heart. Then, he glued a yellow rectangle onto the middle of the hearts, and wrote these words: *Happy Valentine's Day, Mother. I Love You.* How proud he was of the special gift he had made.

Art time ended. Gordon quickly stuffed the valentine into his desk and took out his reading book. By the end of the day, many books had been taken out of and stuffed into his desk.

When it was time to go home, he remembered the gift he had made. He opened his desk, only to discover something terrible. "My present for Mother is all crumpled up!" exclaimed Gordon.

His friend sitting next to him heard his words and said, "That would not have happened if you had kept your desk more orderly."

His friend's words were true. Now he would have to take his mother a wrinkled valentine. But first he would straighten his desk.

Orderliness at Play

"Thank you, Father! This is what I have always wanted!" Gordon exclaimed. He held up a bright, shiny, new stopwatch.

"Don't lose it, Son. These don't grow on trees," said Father.

During the next few days, Gordon did all kinds of fun things with his watch. He timed how fast birds could fly across his backyard. He discovered that it took over twenty seconds to run around his house.

One day, Gordon became careless about putting his watch in its place. He left it outside, and it disappeared.

I guess Father found my stopwatch and took it away, Gordon said to himself, sadly. *This should teach me to be more orderly. Maybe, if I try extra hard to put my things away, he will give it back to me.*

Gordon became more orderly, but the watch was not returned. Then, one day, Father called him. "Look up in that crow's nest," he said.

There, glimmering in the sun, was his shiny watch. Gordon climbed up into the big oak tree in the front yard. Retrieving his watch, he shouted, "The crow must have found my watch in the yard."

"Did you carelessly leave your watch outside?" asked Father.

"Yes, I did," replied Gordon. "Please forgive me for not being orderly. I will try harder to keep all my things in their proper place."

Discern

fern

Able to See Things As They Really Are

But strong meat belongeth to them that are of full age, even those who by reason of use have their senses exercised to discern both good and evil.

Hebrews 5:14

Discernment in the Bible

"Stand up and come here," commanded Jesus.

All the people turned to look at the man seated in the back of the synagogue. Slowly, he stood and made his way forward. Ashamed, he tried to hide his paralyzed hand under his cloak. All eyes were fixed on the Teacher and the crippled man before them.

Now we will see what this Jesus will do, thought the Pharisees and scribes. *Today is the Sabbath, and our law states that no work must be done. If He heals the man, He is guilty of breaking the law.*

Then Jesus said to them, "I will ask you one thing: Is it lawful on the Sabbath days to do good, or to do evil; to save life, or to destroy it?"

No one answered, not even the wicked religious leaders. Jesus looked at them in grief and in anger. He knew their hearts. He knew their unbelief and hatred.

"Stretch forth your hand," Jesus commanded the crippled man.

From under his cloak, the man put forth a trembling hand. The hand was made instantly whole. The crowd gasped. Quickly, the Pharisees and scribes left the room to plot how to kill Jesus. Then, discerning their intentions, Jesus left the synagogue to continue His ministry.

Discernment at Home

"Vern," called his mother, "Jason telephoned to ask you to go and play with him tonight. Would you like to go?"

"That sounds great!" Vern said happily. "Jason is fun to play with."

When Vern arrived, Jason invited him into the living room, where the television was turned on. "I am glad you could come, Vern," he said. "I am watching an exciting program."

As the boys watched television, Vern became uneasy. He saw that people dressed immodestly. He heard angry shouts and bad language. The program became filled with violence and unkind actions. Vern knew that the program was not pleasing to God.

Politely, Vern asked if he could be excused to go to the playroom. When Jason finished watching the program, he joined Vern.

"Don't you like to watch television?" asked Jason.

"Some things are all right on television," said Vern. "But since I've become a Christian, I don't enjoy watching that kind of program. The Bible says that our eyes are the light of the body. I want to be sure that thoughts entering my mind are pleasing to God. Anger, violence, bad language, and immodest dress do not please God."

"I never thought about television that way," said Jason. "You are showing me how to be discerning."

Discernment at School

Vern closed the book. He did not want to fill his mind with things that were not true.

The library book Vern was reading said the earth took millions of years to become what it is today. It further stated that people evolved from animals. This was strange information. Vern knew it could not be true. The Bible says God made the world in only six days. And the first man, Adam, was made from the dust of the ground.

That evening, Vern asked his father about books. "Father, do some books tell the truth and some books lie?" he asked.

"Well, perhaps you might put it that way," he said. "Not *all* books explain things God's way. You must learn to discern which books are telling the truth. These books are best."

Later that evening, Vern had his father take him back to the library. He took the book to the desk to return it.

"Did you enjoy the book, young man?" asked the librarian.

"The pictures were beautiful," replied Vern. "But as I read, I discerned that the book was not telling the truth about how the world began."

"I'm glad that you were so careful with your mind. Sometimes, it is difficult to forget, once we have read a book. Let's go find a book that will please you and the Lord," said the librarian.

Discernment at Play

"The decision is up to you, Son," cautioned Vern's father. "You must think over each offer carefully before you choose."

Vern had been offered the opportunity to play on two soccer teams in the same league. The Bakersville Rockets were the town's champion team. Most of the team, including the coach, were strangers to Vern. The other team was sponsored by the Christian school he attended. This team was new and needed one more player so it could join the league.

In deep thought, Vern plopped down into a big easy chair to think over his choice. It would be a real honor to play with the Rockets. He was sure the coach was not a Christian, because of the foul language he had used in games last year. On the other hand, his school team would have a Christian coach and players. They really needed Vern to give them enough players to join the league.

The longer he thought, the more he discerned that his best choice would be to support his school team. It would be selfish to join the Rockets because they were champs. Besides, he realized that it would be best to help his school and have Christian companions.

"Father, I have made up my mind to join the school team," Vern said confidently.

"Great, Son," responded Father. "I am glad that you were able to see facts clearly and make up your mind. And I think your choice shows great discernment."

Primary Character Challenges

Here are some practical suggestions that will reinforce the concepts taught in the preceding stories.

Self-Control
1. Encourage the child to form a good, new habit or break an old, bad one.
2. Help the child memorize Philippians 4:13.
3. Have the child draw a picture which illustrates self-control.

Orderliness
1. Orderliness is achieved by having a place for everything. Help the child arrange his desk, closet, or drawer to achieve orderliness.
2. Help the child memorize 1 Corinthians 14:40.
3. Teach the child to set the table, learning the positions of the silverware, plate, and glass or cup. Have the child carry his plate and silverware to the sink after the meal.

Discernment
1. Make a list, with the child, of the things that he should avoid when he views television. Some examples are: violence, anger, dishonesty, foul language, and immodesty.
2. Help the child memorize Hebrews 4:12.
3. Isaiah 7:15 and Romans 12:9 talk about refusing evil and choosing good. Discuss with the child situations in which he should refuse evil and choose good.